THE ANGRY CHRISTIAN

The Living as a Christian series:

Basic Christian Maturity

Growing in Faith
  Steve Clark

Knowing God's Will
  Steve Clark

*Decision to Love: What It Means to Love
Others from the Heart*
  Ken Wilson

*God First: What It Means to Love God
above All Things*
  Ken Wilson

The Emotions

*The Angry Christian: How to Control - and
Use - Your Anger*
  Bert Ghezzi

*The Self-Image of a Christian: Humility and
Self-Esteem*
  Mark Kinzer

**Bert Ghezzi and Peter Williamson
General Editors**

The Angry Christian

How to Control—and Use—Your Anger

Bert Ghezzi

Servant Books
Ann Arbor, Michigan

Published by Servant Books
P.O. Box 8617
Ann Arbor, Michigan 48107

Cover Photo by John B. Leidy,
copyright © Servant Publications
Book Design by John B. Leidy

Scripture quotations are taken from the *Revised
Standard Version*, copyright 1946, 1953, © 1971, 1973
by the Division of Christian Education of the
National Council of the Churches of Christ in the
U.S.A.

Printed in the United States of America

ISBN 0-89283-086-7

Contents

Living as a Christian

In human terms, it is not easy to decide to follow Jesus Christ and to live our lives as Christians. Jesus requires that we surrender our selves to him, relinquish our aspirations for our lives, and submit our wills to God. Men and women have never been able to do this easily; if we could, we wouldn't need a savior.

Once we accept the invitation and decide to follow Jesus, a new set of obstacles and problems assert themselves. We find that we are often ignorant about what God wants of us as his sons and daughters. For example, what does it mean in practical terms to obey the first commandment—to love God with our whole mind, heart, and strength? How can we know God's will? How do we love people we don't like? How does being a Christian affect what we do with our time and money? What does it mean "to turn the other cheek?" In these areas—and many others—it is not easy to understand exactly what God wants.

Even when we do know what God wants, it can be quite difficult to apply his teaching to our daily lives. Questions abound. How do we find time to pray regularly? How do we repair a relationship with someone we have wronged or who has wronged us? How do we handle unruly emotional reactions? These are examples of perplexing questions about the application of Christian teaching to our daily lives.

Furthermore, we soon discover that Christians have enemies—the devil outside and the flesh within. Satan tempts us to sin; our inner urges welcome the temptation, and we find our will to resist steadily eroding.

Finally, we must overcome the world. We are trying to live in an environment that is hostile toward what Christians believe and how they live and friendly toward those who believe and do the opposite. The world in which we live works on our Christian resolve in many subtle ways. How much easier it is to think and act like those around us! How do we persevere?

There is a two-fold answer to these questions: To live successfully as Christians, we need both grace and wisdom. Both are freely available from the Lord to those who seek him.

As Christians we live by grace. The very life of God works in us as we try to understand God's teaching, apply it to our lives, and overcome the forces that would turn us aside from our chosen path. We never stand in need of grace. It is always there. The Lord is with us always, and the supply of his grace is inexhaustible.

Yet grace works with wisdom. Christians must *learn* a great deal about how to live according to God's will. We must study God's word in scripture, listen to Christian teaching, and reflect on our own experience and the experience of others. Many

Christians today lack this kind of wisdom. This is the need which the *Living as a Christian* series is designed to meet.

The book you are reading is part of a series of books intended to help Christians apply the teaching of scripture to their lives. The authors of *Living as a Christian* books are pastoral leaders who have given this teaching in programs of Christian formation in various Christian communities. The teaching has stood the test of time. It has already helped many people grow as faithful servants of the Lord. We decided it was time to make this teaching available in book form.

All the *Living as a Christian* books seek to meet the following criteria:

- **Biblical.** The teaching is rooted in scripture. The authors and editors maintain that scripture is the word of God, and that it ought to determine what Christians believe and how they live.

- **Practical.** The purpose of the series is to offer down-to-earth advice about living as a Christian.

- **Relevant.** The teaching is aimed at the needs we encounter in our daily lives—at home, in school, on the job, in our day-to-day relationships.

- **Brief and Readable.** We have designed the series for busy people from a wide variety of backgrounds. Each of the authors presents profound Christian truths as simply and clearly as possible, and illustrates those truths by examples drawn from their experience.

* **Integrated.** The books in the series comprise a unified curriculum on Christian living. They do not present differing views, but rather they take a consistent approach.

The format of the series makes it suitable for both individual and group use. The books in *Living as a Christian* can be used in such group settings as Sunday school classes, adult education programs, prayer groups, classes for teenagers, women's groups, and as a supplement to Bible study.

The *Living as a Christian* series is divided into several sets of books, each devoted to different aspects of Christian living. These sets include books on Christian maturity, emotions in the Christian life, the fruit of the Holy Spirit, Christian personal relationships, Christian service, and very likely, on other topics as well.

This book, *The Angry Christian*, is part of a set covering the emotions in the Christian life. The nature of modern society forces us to be more concerned about our emotions than our Christian ancestors had to be. Not that they were unemotional. Ironically, they were more expressive of their emotions than most of us are. But nowadays we look at our emotions differently, and the instability of relationships and pressures of modern life introduce some new problems. *The Angry Christian* and other books in this set present a practical scripturally-based strategy for emotional health.

The editors dedicate the *Living as a Christian* series to Christian men and women everywhere who have counted the cost and decided to follow Jesus Christ as his disciples.

Bert Ghezzi and Peter Williamson
General Editors

ONE

The Anger Reaction

Recently, my wife and I were having dessert at Annie's, a restaurant near our home. In the summer, Annie's is usually too noisy for conversation, because boisterous players and fans from the nearby ball fields crowd in for refreshments after games. Once softball season is over, things tend to quiet down. That night we had enjoyed a pleasant talk, a snack, and the service of a friendly waitress.

As we were about to leave, a man began to shout at a young waiter. The fellow had been drinking, perhaps too much, and something the waiter said had triggered his rage. "Where's the manager?," the irate patron demanded. "I know the owner," he threatened, "and he'll hear about this." All conversation stopped. The waiter and the customers that remained, including us, watched the man with some trepidation. He paced back and forth in the aisle between the booths and the counter, alternately muttering to himself, seeking agreement from another customer and behaving abusively toward the waiter. We were all afraid he might strike the young man or vent his fury in some act of violence. Eventually he left the building, but not without roaring a final imprecation.

This scene at Annie's provides a dramatic, though not uncommon, example of what can happen when someone loses his temper. I observed in it some interesting and instructive facts about anger. In the first place, I was struck by the power that anger generated for the angry man. Something had not gone the way he had wanted. He became angry and exploded, but it must be said that his rage was getting him through frustrating circumstances. Anger was controlling him and he was controlling the situation, because the waiter and everyone else were afraid of what he might do.

Secondly, I reflected on the fear that we all experienced. In part, it was a natural reaction, a warning that danger was near. For me, and the other customers, too, I think, it also came from remembering how anger has drawn me on occasion toward the brink of irrational behavior. Our common fear spoke of our familiarity with this powerful emotion. Is there anyone who has lost his temper who has not wondered what he might do under the influence of so wild and furious a passion?

Everybody Gets Angry

There are many people nowadays who believe that our feelings are what make us unique. I could not disagree more. Events like the erruption at Annie's persuade me, to the contrary, that the experience of emotions is not unique to individuals but the same for all. I recognized anger in the enraged customer because I had made its acquaintance before in myself. I identified fear in the young waiter because it matched my own. Like feet, hands, muscles, sight, speech and thought, emotions are part of the standard operating equipment of human beings. No, feelings do not make us unique. In fact, we have them in common. They make us alike.

The anger reaction is familiar to all. When something goes wrong, or does not go our way, a surge of emotion rises in us. Adrenalin flows into the bloodstream. Muscles tense. Pulse quickens— bodies instinctively prepare to respond. In the crescendo of rising anger we recognize a force within that has the power to dominate. Something has been aroused in us that seems to have the potential, if unleashed, to consume an adversary. And if not released, we think at times that it may destroy us from within.

Anger involves both an inner reaction and an outward response. The two movements are so intertwined as to be virtually indistinguishable. This is not readily apparent to all, for the modern tendency is to focus on the feeling apart from the related external behavior.

Responses to anger vary considerably but fall into definable categories. Sometimes, like our friend at Annie's, we lose our temper. Voices become increasingly shrill until they break into shouting. Impassioned desires to lash out occasionally find fulfillment in a coming to blows.

Violent expression of anger may climax in hostility, enmity and even murder. Other expressions of anger include irritability, negativity, resentment and depression.

Irritability

One day last week my wife went shopping at a catalog discount store. She was looking for a boy's wristwatch that had been advertised at a very reduced price. Salespersons were at a premium, as they always are in this type of store. Finally she got the attention of a young lady to assist her. As it turned out the girl gave only grudging help. When my wife, who shops with the thoroughness of a research chemist, requested to see other watches, she sighed and clapped them out on the counter. "How long will this battery last?" my wife asked. "I really don't know," came the exasperated reply. The tone of voice seemed to say, "Lady, how am I supposed to know?" This salesperson was angry, and she was expressing it in irritability.

Irritable people are often described as grumpy or touchy. Their demeanor communicates to all that they are at the very limit of their patience and at the next provocation they may errupt. They are short with people, when they're communicating at all. They express dissatisfaction with sighs or a click of the tongue. If someone asks an obvious question, their answer says between the lines, "How could anyone be so stupid?" Irritable people are disagreeable and seem, perversely, to take pleasure in disagreement.

Negativity

Ten years ago, when I was employed as a college professor, I had a colleague whom I can best characterize as being habitually critical. I am well aware that cynicism is a common by-product of the quest for advanced degrees, but this person possessed the trait to excess. In the car on the way to work, this professor's criticalness customarily set the tone for work relationships during the day. "This is weather?!" she would ask, mockingly, as she climbed into the auto on blustery mornings. Then she would lead her companions through her repertory of complaints: the town was provincial, the students were illiterate, the academic vice-president was a simpleton and the governor of the state an idiot. This woman's tone was contagious; it brought out negativity in me and our other associates. While other factors were also at work, during the period of a year her negative disposition helped to divide our once congenial department into two opposing camps. As I got to know this professor over a three-year period, I could see that the root of her perpetual negativity was perpetual anger. Among other things, she was fundamentally miffed that, despite superb credentials from a prestigious eastern graduate school, she had to be satisfied with teaching at a struggling state college that nobody ever heard of.

Negativity is one way of expressing anger. We sometimes see a form of it in the child who expresses hurt or disappointment by teasing his peers unkindly. Or we see it in the person who tells negative jokes that communicate more frustration than humor: The phone rings, "Is John handy?" the caller inquires. "No, John isn't handy at all," replies his workmate, "but he's right here. I'll put him on." Negativity is hostility stored just below the surface, where it can lash out in negative humor, sarcasm, criticism or some other form. Like other manifestations of anger, it often results in broken or unfriendly relationships.

Resentment

Father Jim is a Roman Catholic priest who spent many dedicated years serving his congregation. He was dutiful and efficient. Under his capable direction his modestly prosperous parish had built a handsome church and maintained a parochial school. As I got to know this man I discovered that anger was a big problem for him. The root of his difficulty was resentment.

A series of changes seemed to him to derail his ministry and his plans. He resented this deeply, and his resentment was directed toward all those who seemed to bring on the changes.

His early tenure as pastor had been relatively peaceful. But later, events conspired to complicate his life. The religious order that had staffed the school had to withdraw their teachers. He had the unpleasant task of closing down the school. In the process, many of his old friends opposed him. At the same time, he had been told to establish a parish council. He grudgingly complied, but involving laymen in decision-making upset the routines he had instituted. His anger smoldered in resentment, and everybody suffered from it, including himself.

Resentment is anger that comes from holding a grudge. Someone hurts us, and we desire to redress our grievance by hurting them back. Anticipation of the revenge is perversely delicious. In our imagination we may plot vengeful actions in vivid detail.

The resentful person rarely conceals his anger. It bristles menacingly when he is around his offender. He may even pull off the anticipated revenge and harm the person who harmed him. He is always the worse for it himself, because resentment invariably injures its bearer more than its object.

Depression

My wife and I became acquainted with an effervescent young lady at various church meetings about ten years ago. Several times Virginia spent pleasant evenings with our young family. On these occasions she was jolly, laughed a lot, and was eager to be helpful. About six months after we met her, she went away to school. Before the year was up, Virginia was back in town, and she was not in very good shape emotionally.

Friends from our church invited Virginia to live with their large family. They expected that the support and affection of their family would drive away her unhappiness. For a brief time her spirits lifted, but, within two weeks after moving in,

Virginia became very depressed. She isolated herself from the family. She became incommunicative and would spend days on end in her room. The lady of the house could sense rage boiling beneath the surface and was afraid to try to draw her into family activities.

Virginia was suffering from a severe depression. The root of her problem was anger—anger with her father who had abandoned her mother and her when she was an infant; anger with God who had allowed it to happen; and anger with herself, who had handled many things badly.

Depression may be a symptom of other physical or emotional difficulties. But in many cases people who withdraw are acting in response to anger. Anger-bred depression leads people to unsocial behavior like giving others the cold shoulder or deliberately faulting on a commitment. In more severe forms, it can lead to serious emotional and spiritual problems and result in violence against others and oneself.

For most human beings, anger has been a bad experience. Seldom do we know how to use it constructively. Our track record may list one failure after another. We are embarrassed that we repeatedly lose our temper. We feel guilty about the quarrels provoked by our irritability. We suppress angry feelings and hurt others through our negative behavior. The more we get angry the worse we feel about ourselves. Mishandling anger leads to other emotional problems. And in its wake it leaves a trail of broken friendships. Small wonder that most of us have concluded that anger is a negative, even destructive emotion.

We have all heard endless advice on how to deal with anger, ranging from folk wisdom to technical theories. "My mother used to say, 'when angry count to ten.' So I count to ten, *then* I blow my stack." My bet is that those who actually count to ten, pause; then, not knowing what to do with the anger, they push it down.

Racks of self-help books are available at the nearest supermarket to help us look out for "number one's" emotions. Modern secular counselors and some of their Christian counterparts instruct us to let our anger out. Confront the offender, punch or kick some pillows, scream if that helps. On the other hand, we find Christians instructing us to avoid anger as much as possible, hinting that being angry without sinning is next to impossible. Popular, too, is Christian teaching which recommends that we daily pursue the healing of angry memories.

Advice abounds, but the question remains: what ought a person do with anger? In your hands is yet more advice designed to help you understand anger. This advice contains a simple, biblically-based strategy for getting anger to work right instinctively. I present it confidently not only because of its roots in scripture, but also because it has worked in the lives of thousands who have taken the approaches recommended in the following chapters.

TWO

The Tiger in My Basement

For seven years I taught history at a state college whose students came mostly from the surrounding counties. They were serious, hard-working and average. I enjoyed teaching them, since many could be inspired to high achievement. When an excellent student appeared, he was literally a standout, and teachers could be expected to take notice.

Once, while grading quarterly exams for a senior college course, I found myself awarding an A to a student I did not know. He had written a superb essay on the French Revolution. I was surprised I had not discovered him sooner. The next day I made it a point to identify and meet him.

The student turned out to be a quiet, respectful young man who lived with his family on a farm only a few miles from the college. He never spoke up in class. Even when I called on him, he was barely able to contribute to the discussion. At first, I thought he was shy and reserved. But as I got to know him during the next two years, it became plain that his problem was not shyness.

We had a number of conversations in my office. He seemed to like to visit, but found conversing about himself very painful. Now and then he simply responded with silence, as though he had nothing to say, but he was just clamming up.

Beneath a front of exterior quiet, rage festered inside this bright young man. For reasons he withheld, he was furious with his father. Through nineteen years he had doggedly disciplined himself to shove the anger down. Day by day he had tenaciously built a lid over his volcano. He responded to the hostile internal churning by repressing it and making himself impenetrable to other people.

Keeping the Lid On

Repression is the most common response people make to feelings of anger. This response is even more typical than outbursts of temper. Something goes wrong, or something does not go the way we want, or somebody hurts us; an angry reaction wells up in us; we get a firm hold on the anger and push it down.

Past experience provides us with rationale for repressing our anger. Others may have responded to our angry outbursts with even greater anger. Our parents may have tolerated no expression of anger whatsoever. Our fits of temper may have led to quarrels and cost us friendships. Anger may have caused us to behave in ways that embarrassed us. We may tend to such violence when under its influence that we are afraid to express it lest we lose control. Shame, punishment, dissension and rage—either ours or someone else's—are unpleasant prospects, so we frequently decide to keep our anger to ourselves.

Christians who habitually repress their anger often do so out of a conviction that expressing anger is always sinful. This notion is very common among Christians. It is reinforced by the experience of all the behavior and relationship problems that angry outbursts seem to generate.

What's more, selected scripture texts can be cited to justify the approach. Those who think anger is simply wrong point to Galatians 5:20 where Paul lists anger as a work of the flesh along with sexual immorality, idolatry, envy and other serious offenses. And when Paul ordered the Colossians (3:8) and Ephesians (4:31) to put away anger, was he not prescribing repression as the right means for dealing with anger? Thus, the Bible can seem to support the conviction that anger is sinful in itself and to indicate that repression is the right way for Christians to handle it. As we shall see, both are mistaken conclusions.

Repression Means Trouble

If repression were an effective response to angry feelings, most of us would enjoy a greater measure of emotional health and more peaceful personal relationships. But bottled-up anger is anger waiting for an outlet.

Imagine if you will, the following predicament. A man comes home from work one day and discovers to his horror that a tiger has moved into his house. With a mighty effort the man overcomes his initial fear, lures the tiger into the basement, and slams the door. To ensure the beast's confinement he pushes the refrigerator against the door and heaves a great sigh of relief. "That takes care of that," he says to himself.

Shortly, however, menacing sounds stir in the basement. Loud roars alternate with ferocious tearings at the door. The whole house rumbles as the beast vents his fury in devastation.

The next-door neighbor telephones to inquire about the strange noises. "Oh, nothing to be alarmed about," says the man, hoping to cover up the facts. "The man from the heating company told me to expect my old furnace would be growling this winter. It needs to be replaced." "I wonder what I'll tell the neighbors in July?" he thinks. Next, the paperboy refuses to make deliveries because, twice, he was brushed by a huge paw reaching out a window.

What is the man going to do when the inevitable happens? Either someone will discover his terrible secret, or the tiger will lash out and harm someone, or new tigers wil show up and compound the problem.

When we push anger down, we are like the man in this vignette. But we have only postponed expressing it. Like the tiger in the basement, it begins to cause trouble for us. It constantly stalks the walls of its confinement looking for ways to break out. Neighbors think they hear muffled noises or claim to have dodged a menacing gesture. "No, everything is all right," we assure them, attempting to conceal the obvious. Everybody knows that something is wrong. Some have seen the anger break out. Others detect its unfriendly presence in our behavior.

Many people go through life unhappy because they have decided to keep tigers in the basement. Worse, some people, like my former student, develop serious emotional problems as the result of habitually repressing their anger.

Simply stated, repression does not deal with anger effectively. In fact, pushing it down does not deal with anger at all. Repressed anger is anger unexpressed. Because it does not work, repression disqualifies itself as a proper way to respond to anger.

THREE

"I Feel, Therefore, I Am"

Another method of handling anger has gained enormous popularity in this the "Age of Following Your Feelings." Secular counselors have redefined human nature, identifying being with feeling. One popular representative of this view, Dr. David Viscott writes: "Living in our feelings, we are most in touch, most alive. To paraphrase Descartes, there is nothing more true than "I feel, therefore, I am'"[1]

Feelings, says this modern view, are givens, fundamental personal realities that must be accepted. Happiness comes from following our feelings; if we attempt to control or change them, the result is misery. An increasing number of Christians in search of emotional wholeness have adopted this understanding and have uncritically and contradictorily combined it with Christian teaching on the subject. Anger, described in this perspective as a powerful negative emotion, must be expressed openly. Relief comes to the angry man only when the anger locates and redresses the original hurt.

Advice based on this approach varies, but leads in the same direction: Be honest! "Own" your anger. Express it overtly. Confront the individual who hurt you. Tell it like it is. Make others aware of how you feel. Don't let them wiggle out of it.

If for some reason confrontation is not possible, popular counselors prescribe other methods of letting anger out. Dr. Viscott, again:

> Imagine the person who has offended you dressed in ridiculous disguises, such as red tights and feathers....A ridiculous fantasy helps dissipate anger nicely and will put a smile on your face that will drive the other person absolutely crazy. Besides, the other person is already wearing a ridiculous disguise by being an angry person. Your fantasy will help you put that into perspective.
>
> ....You can telephone the offending person keeping the button down, and let all your anger out. Anything that will put you in imaginery contact and release your feelings will work very nicely. Even if you feel silly, try it....Pounding a pillow for ten minutes also provides tremendous release....So does screaming. But be careful, these devices can become ends in themselves and should only be used as a substitute for the real thing when the actual person is unavailable or you haven't yet worked up the courage and ability to confront him directly.[2]

Dr. Viscott's recommendations are guarded and moderate compared to the practice of some of his colleagues and some sensitivity groups.

Unhealthy Expression

Recently a man I know sought the advice of a local psychotherapist. The counselor invited him to participate in one of his group sessions. My friend, who genuinely needed help, attended a meeting that lasted four hours. Each of eight male and female participants had about half-an-hour to share. One after another they took turns working themselves into a lather over their problems, letting out their anger by striking imaginary opponents, kicking objects, cursing and shouting. The man stayed through the session. His experience there convinced him that venting anger in this fashion did not seem very helpful.

Many counselors specifically recommend to patients that they release their anger by striking or punching an object that represents the person they are angry with. "Patients may regard it (a punching bag) as the trunk or head of a person... It can be made to represent the object of the patient's hostility."[3] Pastors are advised in an article on "Practical Pastoral Counseling" that, "The counselor may invite him to punch a pillow held by the counselor, or lay down on a chair or sofa, or play a game of darts on the board on which any VIP...may be projected."[4] The goal of such behavior is to enable the individual to express anger without restraint in real-life situations.

It must be said in fairness that the follow-your-feelings approach to anger is based upon the correct perception that repression does not deal with anger effectively. However, the prescriptions of the follow-your-feelings movement do not work either.

Anger Generates More Anger

Expressing anger indiscriminately fails to resolve it. A person does not need to be promiscuous to make the commonsense observation that ordinary sexual experience tends to stimulate sexual desire. And anger, like sexual desire, increases rather than decreases when indulged without discipline.

Even when expressed under control, anger may generate more of its kind. I observed a person, quite rightly I think, angrily reprove a newspaper columnist who had slandered him. The individual explained to me later that he did not feel very angry at the moment, but expressed himself hotly to convince the journalist of her wrongdoing. He left the meeting, and as he climbed into his car, which momentarily blocked traffic, a taxi driver announced his impatience by leaning on his horn. The man, overcome with anger, growled, "I'd like to go back and punch his lights out." His controlled expression of anger had induced an inappropriate and intemperate reaction.

How much more anger results from promiscuously letting it all hang out by punching pillows and shrieking obscenities? The follow-your-feelings people admit in print that their approach inclines to excess. One of the frankest, Jane Howard has written: "Most of the angry gestures amounted to ritual murders. Many people had to be reminded: "Remember, it's only a pillow!'"[5]

Admissions such as this indicate that even if it worked to let anger out, Christians would have to be extremely wary of the method. Uncontrolled expression of anger contradicts the scriptural teaching on anger: "Be angry, but do not sin...give no opportunity to the devil" (Eph 4:26). Following your feeling of anger—letting it out of control or putting it in control—leads to grave emotional and spiritual problems. Among these are rage, resentment, hostility, broken relationships and domination by evil spirits.

There is hardly anyone who does not have a friend or relative who has bought into the follow-your-feelings approach. Dignified and reserved people who have patiently struggled with personal problems have been persuaded that their panacea lies in venting their anger. The cure is often worse than the disease. Expressing anger indiscriminately may result in name-calling, name-calling can lead to quarrels, quarrels can degenerate into fights, fights can cause enmity, and enmity can culminate in murder. Better to end up in heaven with some unresolved emotional problems, than to end up in hell because we followed our feelings there.

FOUR

Is Anger Always Sinful?

For every Christian who holds that it's always right to vent anger, I would not hesitate to estimate that there are ten who believe that anger is simply wrong. Some think that expressing anger openly is always sinful. Others extend this perspective to the point where they repent for even having angry feelings. They have not usually thought much about how a Christian should view anger. Anger has gotten them into trouble in the past. They have come to believe that expressed anger is always disruptive. When someone gets angry in their presence, they feel uncomfortable and embarrassed. For them, all overt anger goes hand in hand with obvious wrongdoing like picking fights or cruelty. They know that their anger has caused them to offend people, which they would like to avoid if at all possible. Guilt feelings confirm their experience: "I always feel guilty about anger, so anger must always be wrong."

When we test this view against scripture, we discover that it is mistaken. It must be said, however, before we turn to look at the scriptural teaching on anger, that many modern Christians rarely think of the Bible as a place to find instruction about anger or about any emotion, for that matter. Over the past thirty or forty years the media have trained us to believe that psychologists are the only people who can teach us about emotions. The soap operas and situation comedies, the Sunday supplements and Ann Landers have persuaded us that the way to resolve emotional problems is to get professional help.

Please don't conclude that I disdain psychology and psychologists. To the contrary, I recognize and value their contributions. But I reject the popular misconception that we modern people necessarily understand human nature better than the scriptures. Somehow we have been led to think that Paul, for example, knew far less about human emotions (and many other things about people) than we do. Even if, for the sake of discussion, we set aside his advantage of revelation, Paul had the heritage of many centuries of practical Jewish wisdom on the subject of man and his emotions. What modern improvements in our understanding surpass the wisdom evidenced in the following passage from Proverbs? "A soft answer turns away wrath, but a harsh word stirs up anger" (15:1). That humans have changed all that much and that we know a lot more about them than our forebears are myths borne of the Enlightenment idea of progress.

If we are going to approach anger in a way that corresponds to the Lord's purpose, we must have his instruction on it. First we must comprehend God's teaching on the subject, then we can consult professionals. Their principles and practices are strengthened by subordination to his.

Evidence from Scripture

What does scripture say about anger? First off, no one who has read the Bible can deny that the Lord got angry and expressed it openly and with great forcefulness. Consider the following sampling of texts:

> And the Lord said to Moses, "Go down; for your people, whom you brought up out of the land of Egypt, have corrupted themselves;...they have made for themselves a molten calf, and have worshiped it"....And the Lord said to Moses, "I have seen this people and behold, it is a stiff-necked people; now therefore let me alone, that my wrath may burn hot against them, and I may consume them; but of you I will make a great nation" (Ex 32:7-10).

> While the meat was yet between their teeth, before it was consumed, the anger of the Lord was kindled against the people, and the Lord smote the people with a very great plague
> (Nm 11:33).

> "For behold, the Lord will come in fire, and his chariots like the stormwind, to render his anger in fury, and his rebuke with flames of fire"
> (Is 66:15).

> Yet he, being compassionate, forgave their iniquity, and did not destroy them; he restrained

his anger often and did not stir up all his wrath
(Ps 78:38).

Young's Analytical Concordance to the Bible[6] lists
under the words "anger" and "wrath" hundreds
of additional examples. Christians who think that
anger is simply wrong need to confront these
texts. They must ask themselves whether the
Lord is somehow inconsistent when it comes to
obeying his own laws or whether their own
notion is incorrect.

Jesus, too, got angry and directed his anger
against people who were doing something wrong.

Again he entered the synagogue, and a man
was there who had a withered hand. And they
watched him to see whether he would heal him
on the sabbath, so that they might accuse him.
And he said to the man who had the withered
hand, "Come here." And he said to them, "Is it
lawful on the sabbath to do good or to do harm,
to save life or to kill?" But they were silent. And
he looked around at them with anger, grieved at
their hardness of heart, and said to the man,
"Stretch out your hand." He stretched it out,
and his hand was restored (Mk 3:1-5).

Examples such as this, as well as the Lord's
cleansing of the Temple (Jn 2:13-15) and his angry
reproof of the scribes and Pharisees (Mt 23), teach
plainly that Jesus got angry and expressed it openly.

Responding in anger was not behavior that
Christ reserved to himself. Paul, for example, ad-
dressed Christian communities angrily when they

had to be corrected. His letter to the Galatians was a furious reprimand: "I am astonished that you are so quickly deserting him...." (1:6); "O foolish Galatians! Who has bewitched you...." (3:1); "Tell me, you who desire to be under law, do you not hear the law?" (4:21); "I wish those who unsettle you would mutilate themselves!" (5:12). Either Paul had to repent for the way he wrote or the revealed word of God is expressed in an angry letter (and we don't find Paul repenting for it). The message is clear: God and his sons become angry and express it openly. The Bible shows that it is possible to get angry without sinning.

Danger—Handle with Care

What then are we to make of the passages in scripture that seem to forbid anger outright? "Put to death therefore what is earthly in you: fornication, impurity, passion, evil desire, and covetousness, which is idolatry. On account of these the wrath of God is coming. In these you once walked, when you lived in them. But now put them all away: anger, wrath, malice, slander and foul talk from your mouth" (Col 3:5-8; cf. Eph 4:31 and Gal 5:20). How can you get around that sweeping prohibition? Anger heads the list of things that must be put away to await God's anger.

Taking a passage such as this one alone—failing to hold it in the context of other relevant scriptural teaching—results in a misunderstanding. The Bible does not rule out all anger. "Be angry," Paul instructed the Ephesians, "but do not sin; do not let the sun go down on your anger, and give no opportunity for the devil" (Eph 4:26). Paul is not forbidding anger. He is giving an admonition: anger is dangerous; handle it with care.

The teaching of Proverbs and James supports this view. "He who is slow to anger is better than the mighty, and he who rules his spirit than he who takes a city" (Prv 16:32). "Let every man be quick to hear, slow to speak, slow to anger, for the anger of man does not work the righteousness of God" (Jas 1:19). These passages do not outlaw anger. They warn us to be "slow to anger," teaching us to govern its use rather than to avoid it altogether.

The Lord Jesus himself gives a serious warning about using anger righteously, but he does not forbid it. "But I say to you that everyone who is angry with his brother *without cause* shall be liable to judgment" (Mt 5:21). *Without cause* is a qualifier present in ancient authoritative sources that verify the interpretation advanced here. The Lord is concerned about anger rooted in enmity and leading to murder. This brand of anger is always wrong. And even righteous anger must be expressed warily.

Thus, biblical teaching does not say that anger is always sinful. It prohibits anger that is out of control or in control of us (Prv 16:32; Jas 1:19), or anger resulting in quarrels or dissension (Gal 5:20; Eph 4:26), or anger motivated by hatred or malice (Col 3:8, Eph 4:31, Mt 5:21). But within these biblical boundaries there is considerable room for the righteous expression of anger.

FIVE

When Is Anger OK?

God created anger for us and made it an integral part of our humanity. Along with other powerful emotions, like fear and grief, he designed anger to be a valuable force in our life. Fear alerts us to imminent danger. Grief soothes the agony of great personal loss. Anger is a natural human reaction to obstacles. When we find ourselves in a frustrating situation, an angry reaction instinctively begins to work in us. God intends us to use this surge of emotion. It is meant to mobilize us for accomplishing things that demand effort and to equip us to fight through obstacles to what is right and good.

Righteous Anger

Anger is part of our human makeup and is not wrong in itself. As our review of scripture demonstrated, getting angry is not necessarily a sin. It is sometimes righteous. But how can we tell when our anger is okay and when it is not? Few of us have had any experience of righteous anger. For the most part, we don't know how to handle it in the right way. There is a scripturally based rule of thumb that distinguishes between kinds of anger.

Anger is righteous if it is directed against wrongdoing and is expressed under control. Anger is unrighteous if it is directed against something good; or if it is allowed to get out of control or in control of us; or if it expresses dissatisfaction at not getting our own way.

The scriptural illustrations cited earlier flesh out the distinction. In Mark chapter 3, Jesus finds himself opposed by scribes and Pharisees who are looking for evidence to use against him. Because of their hardness of heart, they interpreted the law in a way that would prevent the healing of deformities on the Sabbath. Jesus plainly identified this as wrong. He became angry and directed his anger at them as he prepared to heal the man with the withered hand.

The Lord's anger was a natural response to a difficult situation, a tool to deal with those who opposed a good act he intended to perform. His anger was righteous in that it was directed against the wrongdoing of the scribes and Pharisees. Mark says that "he looked around at them with anger." This passage describes a deliberate gesture in which the Lord's anger constituted a reprimand. He was in control of his angry response; it was not driving him, nor was it out of control.

A Tool for Good

Until recent years I had never personally experienced the righteous expression of anger. It was not that I never became angry. To the contrary, I got angry a lot, but hardly ever for the right reasons. A turning point occurred when I witnessed someone stir up anger to bring a person to repentance. Over the years, my responsibilities as a leader in several Christian groups put me in situations involving someone's serious personal wrongdoing. One night, several years ago, another leader asked me to accompany him while he talked to someone about a pattern of sinful behavior. The meeting was cordial; the leader discussed the matter fairly; his demeanor was at all times kind and generous, but firm. After about an hour-and-a-half of conversation, the man brushed off the reproof, refused to repent, and resisted my friend's recommendations for change. All of a sudden, just after the man made a polite, but definitive refusal, my friend's demeanor changed dramatically. His face flushed with rage and he raised his voice to a shout: "I am so mad at you I could spit," he roared. "Once again you are rejecting sound advice! Don't you know the ultimate consequences you're bringing on yourself?" The man was obviously unnerved by the display of anger, but he held his ground, repeated his position, albeit shakily, and the meeting ended. However, the next day he began to do the things the leader told him to do to repair his wrongdoing. The long conversation had obviously made its impact by means of the angry concluding statement. I asked my friend if he had gotten so angry that it just burst out. "No," he said, "I was quite frustrated. I decided then that I would stir up anger to motivate the man to act." In this case, his anger moved the other man to repentance.

Anger is righteous when it is expressed in

response to sin and is controlled. Another way to say this is: anger is righteous when it is the loving response in a situation. The Lord commands us to love one another just as he loved us. Determining what this means at particular moments is, of course, not always easy.

Hard things like correction, angry reprimands, or reproof do not at first seem very loving. But love demands the best interest of the other and cannot tolerate the self-destructive consequences that wrongdoing incurs. When someone is entrapped by their sinful behavior, an angry word that brings repentance may be more loving at that moment than a word of kindness.

I have letters in my file in which two women describe an event that illustrates how righteous anger is an expression of love.[7]

The first wrote: "A while ago I was living with a group of Christian women, one of whom had problems with moodiness. The way she related to people would depend on how she was feeling at the time. Often, when she felt depressed or bad about herself, she would withdraw, either physically or in her attitude. She wouldn't respond to encouragement, and when someone sympathized with her, she persisted in being withdrawn. She had told me many times how much she wanted to get over this problem and asked my help.

"One evening several women were working together to clean a kitchen in someone's house to help them out. After a while, I noticed that my friend had quietly slipped away into another room. I knew that she had been having a difficult day, and I was pretty sure that she was having another depressed reaction.

"It made me angry to see that she had left the other women and had given in to feeling bad about herself. In the past, I would have let her alone and chalked it up to forbearance. This time I decided to express my anger to her. We were good friends, so I was confident that my becoming angry with her would not jeopardize our relationship. This was the first time she had seen me get angry and she was shocked. She asked me to forgive her for her behavior."

The other woman in this story described her first reaction and her final understanding of the incident: "I was brooding and feeling a lot of self-pity. I went off to be alone and cry. My friend followed me and proceeded to become very angry. She told me that I needed to change my attitude, get my emotions under control and go back and join the group. The anger took me by such surprise that it quickly jolted me into realizing my behavior was wrong.

"I did go back and join the other women that night, but it took a couple of days to work through my reactions to the anger my friend had expressed. My first reaction was to feel rejected and unloved, which was how I had always reacted to anger before. I had always felt personally attacked. But I came to see as I prayed about it that my friend had precisely been acting out of love when she became angry. She got angry simply because she wanted to do everything she could to help me become a more godly woman and didn't stop short of becoming angry to do it."

The first woman writes that since the night of the angry correction, her friend "has made real progress in overcoming her moods. Rather than seeing herself as the victim of these emotional ups and downs, she knows that by grace and her own effort she can overcome them."

Both women learned that night how anger can be the most loving response in a situation.

Another illustration of how to discern righteous anger comes from common childrearing practices. It is a principle in some circles that a parent should never discipline a child "out of anger." This is true if it means that a parent ought not act against his child if his anger is out of control, or is founded simply on a desire to impose his will, or is merely a function of his personal disturbance. But many parents mistakenly believe that they should always refrain from disciplining a child when they are reacting in anger to the child's wrongdoing. This approach harms the parent and deprives the child. Supressed anger hurts the parent; expressed anger would benefit a naughty child by helping him correct his behavior.

Even Dr. Benjamin Spock, who has been widely criticized for his permissive approach to child-raising, makes this point well when he discusses a father's role in discipline:

> If the boy is doing something that makes him cross, the father tries to conceal his feelings and says nothing. This is trying too hard to be

agreeable (or to pretend to be agreeable). A child knows when he has displeased a parent or broken a rule, and he expects to be corrected. If his parent tries to hide his disapproval or irritation, it only makes the child uneasy. He imagines that all this suppressed anger is piling up somewhere (which isn't too far from the truth) and worries about what will happen if it ever breaks out. Child-guidance clinic studies show clearly that the boy whose father declines to do his share in maintaining discipline is much more apt to be afraid of him than the one whose father has no hesitation in controlling his child and showing indignation when it is justified. In the latter cases, the boy pays the price of his misbehavior, learns that though it isn't pleasant it isn't fatal, either, and the air is cleared...[8]

My own experience with my youngest son bears this out. At age 4½ Peter was having trouble with honesty, that is, he was telling lies. After I noticed that he was doing it often and that fibs were swelling into lies, I had a man-to-boy talk with him. In the course of our talk, I deliberately let myself get angry. "Look me in the eyes, Peter," I said sternly. Then I said firmly and angrily: "I will not tolerate lying. From today on lying is a spankable offense. Do you understand?!" He understood. In the next few months, I had to spank him twice, perhaps three times, to underscore the message. At those times, I made it a point to show him that I was very angry with him. In each case my anger was scrupulously righteous. It was directed against Peter's sin and I was in control. Over two years have gone by and the problem has disappeared. Clearly, my anger has helped Peter to stop lying.

Overt expressions of anger are sometimes right, loving and necessary for Christians. Telling a person about their wrongdoing, letting them know we are angry about it, can engage their will for repentance.

This does not constitute acquiescence in the follow-your-feelings approach. It is hard to see how "letting it all out" could be done under control and, therefore, how it could be righteous. Speaking out in anger about something simply because we do not like it and are having a reaction, is not appropriate Christian behavior. Nor is losing our temper or otherwise being out of control. Even an internal angry reaction out of proportion to the situation or directed against something good is not proper for a Christian.

SIX

Anger and
Fruit of the Spirit

Our limited view of anger and the various ways we can express it prevents us from getting angry more often, for the right reasons, in the right way. We restrict our repertory of responses either to repression or to overt manifestations, usually of the unrighteous variety.

This narrowing of alternatives impoverishes us. On the one hand this perspective frequently deprives us of the benefits of anger. Instead of our anger helping us through obstacles, we push it down so that we get an upset stomach, or we let it all out and make enemies in the process. Confining anger to overt—usually negative—expressions, inhibits our Christian growth. For there are expressions of anger, usually neglected, that are effective ways to acquire the fruit of the Holy Spirit.

Strengthening Christian Character

The assertion that anger can act as a powerful catalyst to help us become more like Jesus Christ startles many Christians. The notion that anger can strengthen Christian character seems contradictory to people whose anger has often led them to unchristian behavior. How can anger have anything to do with holiness?

Between repression and explosion there exists a whole range of ways to express anger. Some of these, such as meanness or sarcasm, are wrong and should be avoided. But anger can also be channeled into positive behavior, such as patience, endurance or fight. All of these are marks of Christian character described in scripture. They could correctly be called fruit of the Holy Spirit. As we learn to channel anger constructively, we will be able to get angry without sinning, and our anger will promote our growth in the image of Christ.

Constructive channeling of anger might at first appear to be a disguise for repression. This would be a mistaken judgment. Repression is sheerly a matter of willpower; channeling anger involves the Holy Spirit. Later chapters will present a strategy for anger that will shed more light on this distinction. For now, suffice it to say that the two are not the same.

Patience

Patience, in the scriptural sense of the word, provides an excellent channel for anger. In ordinary speech, patience often means putting up with all sorts of things that really ought not be tolerated. This brand of patience is more akin to Stoic resignation than it is to the scriptural variety. The Stoic's philosophy was to insulate himself so that nothing would affect him. His isolation reflected a passivity that is alien to Christianity.

For the Christian, patience is more like determination. It contains a strong sense of working hard at something until the goal is reached—a sense of persistent application. The meaning is plain in specific texts: "For he will render to every man according to his works: to those who by patience in well-doing seek for glory and honor and immortality, he will give eternal life" (Rom 2:6-7). "Show the same earnestness in realizing the full assurance of hope until the end, so that you may not be sluggish, but imitators of those who through faith and patience inherit the promises" (Heb 6:11-12). Patience, in these two New Testament passages, contains a strong, active element, moving the man who possesses it through obstacles until he achieves his purpose.

The first Book of Maccabees provides a further illustration from ancient political history. Here it is said that the Romans made themselves the masters of the province of Spain by patience (1 Mc 8:4). They persisted in the conquest, keeping at it until they possessed the country, "despite its great distance from their own" (JB).

We needn't look far afield for examples of how anger can be channeled into patience. My children's table manners—or more precisely, their lack of table manners—has in the past been a source of irritation to me. Once I placed my 2½ year-old's high chair behind me to avoid having to watch him eat spaghetti, much to the amusement of our guests. I intended that move to be humorous. But that same child's failure over the next eight years to eat more civilly at supper was a daily aggravation and no joke to me. At age 10, I sat him right beside me so I could supervise his eating habits. "Don't use your fingers!" I would say irritably. "Use your fork I said!" "Don't wipe your hands on your pants! What do you think napkins were made for?" Irritation quickly boiled into uncontrolled anger. "You know you shouldn't reach across someone else's plate. That's rude! Will you ever learn to eat like a human instead of an animal?!" This scene was repeated more often than I like to recall, until a good friend of mine pointed out that this anger was pointless. He showed me that I was venting my anger and disturbing the peace of my table without bringing about any change.

Furthermore, our conversation brought home to me that there were other, more serious things in my son's life and in our relationship that weren't right and ought to change. On his side, my son was constantly provoking his brothers and sisters by teasing them. And there was more than a tinge of rebellion in his response to my efforts to correct him. For my part, I was always on his back. If I wasn't harping to him about how he ate, I was complaining about the way he kept his room or about his failure to do his chores well. It seemed that the whole substance of our conversation had become one altercation after another. While I loved him very much, his behavior and my anger—each magnifying the other—were driving us apart.

On my friend's suggestion, I decided to express the anger I felt toward this son differently. Venting it pointlessly had never changed the situation, so I decided to call a unilateral ceasefire. I began to direct all of my anger into a firm resolve to improve my relationship with my son. I stopped carping at him for the things I did not like about his ways and personal habits. I attempted to correct him only for the serious offenses we had always outlawed: disobedience, willfully hurting another, lying. When I got frustrated with his table manners, I reminded myself of my resolution to work on more important elements in our relationship. Occasionally, if I slipped and lost control (or as my son would say, "Dad blew a hairy"), I repented to him. This would underscore what I had already told him numerous times: I loved him and I was determined to have a good relationship with him. I looked for daily ways to express approval and affection toward him. This was not easy, because much about him still irritated me. But over a few months, as I refrained from constantly correcting and criticizing him, it became easier.

My new resolve led me to make time in my day for this son. If one of my highest priorities was to improve the way I related to him, I realized that I had to invest something considerable in it. We began playing racketball and other sports together regularly. He liked this, because he intends to be a professional in two or three sports at least. We have also begun taking time most evenings to talk over how the day has gone.

This process continues. I still get angry with my son, and I still channel it into determination to maintain our relationship on solid ground.

Occasionally, I have vigorously expressed my anger to him in order to disengage him from some serious wrongdoing. It has worked much better since I have reduced the amount of anger I send his way significantly. On the whole, patience is winning the day for my son and me, just as it won Spain for Rome. The anger that at one time was destroying our relationship has been channeled into a force that helps to build it.

Endurance

Endurance is another channel for anger. It is a quality that enables us to stand firm when under attack. The Hebrew Christians were exhorted to endure:

> But recall the former days when, after you were enlightened, you endured a hard struggle with sufferings, sometimes being publicly exposed to abuse and affliction, and sometimes being partners with those so treated. For you had compassion on the prisoners, and you joyfully accepted the plundering of your property, since you knew that you yourselves had a better possession and an abiding one. Therefore do not throw away your confidence, which has a great reward. For you have need of endurance, so that you may do the will of God and receive what is promised" (Heb 10:32-36).

The Lord's prescription for the sufferings that come to us because of faithfulness is endurance.

"You will be delivered up," Jesus promised, "even by parents and brothers and kinsmen and friends, and some of you they will put to death; you will be hated by all for my name's sake. But not a hair on your head will perish. By your endurance you will gain your lives" (Lk 21:16-19).

Although it is not listed in the principal text (Gal 5:22), endurance can be called a fruit of the Holy Spirit. Endurance comes by the action of the Holy Spirit, inspiring and directing us to persist when trials would otherwise overwhelm us. Paul prays for the Colossians that they may "be strengthened with all power, according to his glorious might, for all endurance and patience with joy..." (Col 1:11). Without the Holy Spirit, we would be left to face hard struggles with our own meager resources. Not many of us would be able to endure for long.

When we are opposed, anger automatically flares up in us. We ought to expect this, since anger is a natural reaction to threats or harm. Venting anger in some such cases may effectively ward off the adversary. When we are under a sustained attack because we are Christian or because of Christian behavior, expressing anger may do some temporary good. But in the long run, venting anger in these situations may worsen matters and cause us to lose ground. Endurance would be more helpful, and that's how we should express the anger we feel in such circumstances.

The Christian students at the state college where I taught were delighted to find professors who were open about their faith. One year I was the faculty adviser to the InterVarsity Christian

Fellowship and to the Newman Center simultaneously. During that time I spoke regularly with a dedicated and spirited young Christian named Scott. He was spunky, aggressive, and had, I think, a big problem with anger. In the winter quarter that year Scott enrolled in an anthropology course that he needed to fulfill a requirement for his social studies major. The professor was a delight to students who were in the process of junking their Christian heritage, for debunking the Christian view of man was one of his specialties. Scott found himself the only Christian in a small discussion class. The professor and Scott's peers caught on quickly. He blew up once in a futile attempt to defend his convictions, which whet the class's appetite for more. Daily they baited him, hoping to provoke repeat performances. Since he was a novice in the discipline, he was no match on intellectual grounds, for the professor too was an antagonist and sided with the rest of the class. Losing his temper lost ground for him, because the class recognized it as unchristian behavior. After several conversations with me in my office, he resolved that he would express his anger through endurance. He decided he would simply study and participate in class to understand what was being taught, without expressing his disagreement. He told the class that he disagreed with them in some very fundamental ways, but that he was going to cease arguing with them during class. He said he was willing to discuss Christianity and his convictions privately with any of them.

The professor and the class did not relent in

their provocations. But with grace he endured. Scott may not have won any intellectual battles that term, but I think his self-control and endurance won the admiration of not a few of his adversaries. He did not lose any battles, either. Endurance helped him hold his ground.

Some opposition comes our way because our Christian behavior differs from the behavior of others around us. Endurance is often the right expression for the anger we experience at these times.

Job situations provide good illustrations of this point. Greg, a close family friend, had taken a job with a subcontractor. He works hard, is intelligent and can oversee others' work. Within a year he had responsibility for a small team of men. For about six months on one particular work site, Greg experienced constant friction with an older, seasoned workman from another company. He seemed to resent Greg's youth, his competence and, above all, his drive. Sometimes this man would leave his work undone, either to complicate Greg's end of the task or to get Greg to do it for him. He did petty things to aggravate him.

It was understandable that Greg was getting angry every day and was often close to losing control. He discussed the situation with his supervisor, but there was no apparent way to change things at that level. He was told that the job would be done in a few months and he should stick it out. Greg tried speaking plainly with the man but got nowhere. He decided that venting his anger would only evoke more of the same from the other and could even result in physical conflict. Greg is not one to run from an assailant, but he judged that in this case he ought not behave in a way that might provoke the man.

Greg chose to channel his anger into endurance. He prayed for the man each morning before work. He disciplined his mind to refrain from imagining revenge. He worked at ignoring pettiness. He did his job energetically. When the other left work undone, Greg worked around it as best he could. Greg did not stop getting angry at the man's behavior. He did find that his anger was no longer plummeting into rage and he could effectively channel it into strength for endurance.

To some it may seem that the notion of channeling anger is only a ruse—a facade for repression. While patience, for example, is not usually an overt expression, it is an expression for anger nonetheless. The literal meaning of the Greek word for patience in the New Testament is "large-tempered" and its opposite is "short-tempered." When a "short-tempered" person confronts an obstacle or is frustrated he responds by losing his temper. A man who encounters the same obstacle and channels his anger into patience settles down to overcome it. When I, for example, channeled the anger I felt toward my son into determination to improve our relationship, I experienced my inner resolve in objective actions. I used my anger fruitfully.

The same holds true for channeling anger into endurance. When Greg was directing his anger into perseverance, he translated his decision into specific activities. Channeling anger into patience or endurance involves an interior resolve that results in specific behavior.

Patience and endurance are two optional expressions for anger. A third is aggressiveness or fight.

SEVEN

Anger and Fight

"I woke up that bright, hot summer morning," Sue explained, "feeling just rotten. My head ached, my sinuses were congested, and I felt awful. Everybody else was making preparations for the picnic at the beach, which we had been planning for weeks. Because of my allergies and everything else, I wasn't up to going along. I forced a smile as I saw them off. Then I sat down on the edge of my bed and began to entertain my old friend, Self-Pity. 'Why does this always happen to me?' I thought. I was so furious and disappointed that I was tempted to crawl between the covers and brood all day. It was a close call. But I had been learning to fight my way out of depression. So I used the anger I was feeling to resist thoughts of self-pity and disappointment. I did feel sick, but not too sick to have a decent day. I got good and mad at the lies that would have messed me up that day. I cleaned up a few dishes; prayed for a while; walked in the park nearby; read a little. When the gang came home that evening, I could say with them, 'It's been a great day!'"

As Sue's testimony shows, anger can also be channeled into fight. Aggressiveness is not found

on New Testament lists of the fruit of the Holy
Spirit, but it is a mode of behavior proper for
Christians. There is a popular misconception that
aggressive behavior is somehow forbidden to the
Christian. Certainly aggression that expressed in-
justice or malice would be sinful. But where do we
find all aggressiveness outlawed? The New Testament instructs us to pay no one evil for evil (Mt
5:38-42; Rom 12:17), but this prohibits revenge, not
aggressiveness. "Do not be overcome by evil,"
Paul taught the Romans, "but overcome evil with
good" (Rom 12:21). In order to respond to wicked-
ness with good behavior, Christians must evidence a good bit of fight. Without it, we would be
milktoasts, completely incapable of resisting evil.

Christ's Example

The Lord himself was aggressive. This contradicts the notion of the soft and sensitive Jesus
popular in some circles that seem to have met
Jesus in the movies instead of the scriptures. It was
an aggressive Jesus—a Jesus consumed with zeal
for this Father's house—who cleansed the Temple
(Jn 2:13-17). Jesus was aggressive even in his own
behalf when he was unjustly attacked: "When he
had said this, one of the officers standing by struck
Jesus with his hand, saying, 'Is that how you
answer the high priest?' Jesus answered him, 'If I
have spoken wrongly, bear witness to the wrong;
but if I have spoken rightly, why do you strike
me?'" (Jn 18:22-23).

Aggressiveness typified Paul's life so much so

that he chose the word "fight" to characterize the course of his Christian service. "I have fought the good fight," he told Timothy. "I have finished the race, I have kept the faith" (2 Tm 4:7).

An Antidote for Fearfulness

Followers of Christ ought to show fight, too, when they encounter unrighteousness. When a Christian comes up against something wrong, he can get angry and fight through it, instead of getting frustrated and depressed.

I have a friend named Mary Ann who provides another good example of channeling anger into fight: "I used to be a 'dove' in all my contacts with people. I was hesitant to state my opinion even in the smallest matters (for example, what I like on a pizza) for fear of offending someone. This was a problem for me.

"The Lord began to change this a few years ago when I had the opportunity to live with a group of Christian women. One of them had a tendency to speak negatively about others. She was a good person and committed to the Lord. I liked most things about her, but this one area was not working right for her, and it was a big difficulty for me.

"At first, when she would complain or speak against someone, I would weakly state the truth or try to combat the negative speech with something positive. The time came when I realized this wasn't working—I think I was being a little too diplomatic about it.

"One day she said something against a mutual

friend. On two previous occasions when she had criticized this person unfairly, I had used the diplomatic approach without success. When I tried it again this time and she kept on speaking about our friend, I got very angry and almost yelled that what she was doing was very wrong and she had better stop it instantly. She was so stunned at my anger that she was speechless. I went away from the situation shaking all over and realized I had not gotten angry in years. Even though I wish I had been a little more controlled, I'm glad I did what I think was the right thing.

"Since that time I have stopped being a dove. I am able to speak up for what is right."

According to her own description, Mary Ann was passive and timid in her relationships. Expressing anger in fight equipped her to speak up against wrongdoing. The first time she did it she seems to have lost her temper. But several years later she is able to oppose wrongdoing without exploding, and anger helps her do it. Channeling her anger into aggressiveness helped Mary Ann overcome a weakness in her character.

Books and training programs in assertive behavior have become very popular in the last few years. With great care and discernment, Christians can learn from the best of these (though much of the literature is open to serious criticism and will be found objectionable to Christians). One of the better books, *Your Perfect Right*[9] by Robert Alberti and Michael Emmons, provides another illustration of how to channel anger into fight.

As a member of the community beautification committee, you are dismayed by the continued dominance of group discussion by Mr. Brown, an opinionated member who has "the answer" to every question. He has begun another tirade. As usual, no one has said anything about it after several minutes.

Alternative responses:

(a) Your irritation increases, but you remain silent.

(b) You explode verbally, curse Mr. Brown for "not giving anyone else a chance," and declare his ideas out-of-date and worthless.

(c) You interrupt, saying, "Excuse me, Mr. Brown." When recognized, you express your personal irritation about Mr. Brown's monopoly on the group's time. Speaking to Mr. Brown as well as the other group members, you suggest a discussion procedure which will permit all members an opportunity to take part and will minimize domination by a single outspoken individual.[10]

Response *a* and *b* are familiar enough as the two most common ways of expressing anger: repression and explosion. Response *c*, described by Alberti and Emmons as assertive behavior is an example of expressing anger in fight. Their interests in *Your Perfect Right* are entirely secular, but this particular element of their approach is consistent with scripture and recommends itself well to Christians. Fight is an antidote to the fear and passivity that prevent Christians from taking a stand when they should.

Patience, endurance and fight expand the range of possible expressions of anger for us. Christians ought to be angry—angry at God's purposes being thwarted, at the drift of evil in the world, at personal wrongdoing. Christians ought to express more anger, overtly and under control, than they do. And when open expression is unwise in some particular situation, we should channel anger into behavior such as determination, steadfastness or aggressiveness. In doing so, we can grow in the fruit of the Spirit, for these marks are among the character traits of Jesus Christ.

EIGHT

Anger Can Change

Modern selfism celebrates the view that, "You are what you feel." Thus, men are led to look to their feelings as the compass for their lives. Feelings are inappropriately elevated and deified, and we are told to follow them as their obedient disciples. The follow-your-feelings approach can aptly be characterized as emotional determinism. Our feelings are givens. Presumably they are cut from some precious substance and placed in us, like diamonds in the mechanism of a watch. We are told that we will be happy, if only we follow them—if we repress them or (worse yet) try to change them—we are doomed to misery.

Centuries of common sense stand against this view. Until the recent past, ordinary people— uneducated and educated alike—have regarded their feelings as valuable natural resources to be governed by man's intellect and will. People moved through their lives and brought their feelings along with them. They paid more attention to ideals, goals, and responsibilities than to how they felt. They were truly other-oriented. They acted on the basis of commitment and right conduct whether or not it felt good to do so.

We ought not presume that people who disciplined their emotions necessarily repressed them and were, therefore, an unhappy lot. The record does not support this view. People in earlier, more traditional societies were far more expressive of their emotions than people are in our industrialized societies. They knew how to express joy, grief and anger instinctively. We have to work at it, because we've forgotten how.

A Personal Revolution

In addition to contradicting common sense, the modern selfist view of emotions is fundamentally opposed to New Testament teaching. The author of life and Christianity presupposed that man could change, that he could be transformed from a being that clings to earth into a god that strides the heavens. Embracing selfism and emotional determinism means rejecting this good news:

> If then you have been raised with Christ, seek the things that are above, where Christ is, seated at the right hand of God. Set your minds on things that are above, not on things that are on earth. For you have died, and your life is hid with Christ in God. When Christ who is our life appears, then you also will appear with him in glory.
>
> Put to death therefore what is earthly in you: immorality, impurity, passion, evil desire, and covetousness, which is idolatry. On account of these the wrath of God is coming. In these you

once walked, when you lived in them. But now put them all away: anger, wrath, malice, slander and foul talk from your mouth. Do not lie to one another, seeing that you have put off the old nature with its practices and have put on the new nature, which is being renewed in knowledge after the image of its creator. Here there cannot be Greek and Jew, circumcised and uncircumcised, barbarian, Scythian, slave, free man, but Christ is all and in all.

Put on then, as God's chosen ones, holy and beloved, compassion, kindness, lowliness, meekness, and patience, forbearing one another and, if one has a complaint against another, forgiving each other; as the Lord has forgiven you, so you also must forgive. And above all these put on love, which binds everything together in perfect harmony (Col 3:1-14).

When people ask me what scripture says about emotions, I refer them to passages like this one from Colossians. The passage teaches that God has changed the Christian. He has died to mere earthliness and has risen in Christ, where he lives in a glorious, godly life. Not only is the Christian radically changed, but the revolution continues. He is commanded to *put* to death earthly wrongdoing and to *put* away every variety of evil behavior. He is instructed that he has put off the old nature, like dirty clothes, and has been clothed afresh in the shining garment of a new nature that is still "being renewed in knowledge after the image of its creator." He is ordered to *put* on the fruit of the Holy

Spirit. Texts that speak of dying and rising, putting off the old and putting on the new, indicate that God expects man and all his parts, including his emotions, to change.

This truth frees the Christian from the bondage of emotional determinism. We are not bound to follow our feelings, because if they are not working right, we can get them to change. If a Christian claims he is irascible by nature and simply cannot control his temper, he is not facing reality. If another says he is simply an irritable person, and that others should tiptoe about him or pay the inevitable consequences, he is misguided.

The truth is that anger can change. A Christian can learn how to change the responses he makes to angry feelings. He can train himself to express his anger in some acceptable way, instead of repressing it or "letting it all out." It will take grace, work and time, but an angry Christian can shed his irascibility and put on a more peaceful disposition. The man himself can be changed at the roots so that he is not given to fits of temper or bouts of depression.

Servant, Not Slavemaster

The idea is to get anger to change so that it works right, not to get it to stop. Only one thing can stop us from feeling anger, or any emotion, and that's death. This is the fact that tripped up those Stoics, who thought they could only be happy by distancing themselves from situations that affected their emotions. The Lord made anger for man, and he wants us to get angry, to feel it intensely and to express it vigorously and righteously.

Feelings of fear or guilt ought not prompt us to repress anger or to indulge in depression. We should be able to communicate anger to someone without losing control. We should have an assortment of instinctive responses ready to manifest our anger.

In short, the Christian should expect anger to be his *servant*. A servant helps, and anger should help the Christian by supporting him in doing the right thing in every situation. A servant follows directions, and anger should be subordinate to the Christian, and not vice versa. A servant anticipates needs by instinct, and anger ought to serve the Christian instinctively, without his having to deliberate about it.

For a Christian, the Holy Spirit and the Body of Christ are the primary sources of personal change. How they work to transform men and women to the core is the subject of the next two chapters.

NINE

Self-Help or God-Help?

People who have problems with anger want to change, but often they do not know how. The mushrooming popularity of self-help books, programs, and seminars attests to this fact. Sometimes people stumble across some good advice and find relief. Sometimes, however, the self-help books cause them to stumble. The fact is that *self*-help is only half the answer because it is a half-truth.

The Christian strategy for getting anger to work right differs in principle from self-help approaches. It would not be inaccurate to call it a "God-help" approach. For a Christian, getting anger or any emotion to change requires a lot more God-help than self-help. If we focus too much on the emotion and invest too much effort in trying to make it go differently, we are courting failure. Most of the work that must happen to free us from emotional problems is the work of the Holy Spirit.

Normal Christianity

By definition, every Christian has the Holy Spirit living in him. God has done what no one else could ever do. He has adopted us by reaching back into time and altering our genealogy, so that sons and daughters of Adam and Eve have truly become sons and daughters of God himself. Because of our sonship, "God has sent the Spirit of his son into our hearts, crying 'Abba, Father' (Gal 4:6).

Normal Christianity, then, means having the Holy Spirit in residence. This is not to be taken casually, though I am afraid we often do. The Spirit of God—the source of life that brooded over the creation of everything from nothing, the same Spirit of God, who conquered death by restoring the crucified Jesus to life (Rom 8:11)—dwells in us, bringing us dynamic new life. He inspires prayer, opens the mysteries of God to us, gives us wisdom for daily living, equips us to build the church with gifts such as prophecy and healing, overcomes our personal habits of wrongdoing and in their place produces his fruit in us: the character traits of Jesus Christ himself.

Yielding to the Holy Spirit

Thirteen years ago, when I first encountered these facts and took them seriously, I judged that my own Christian life was subnormal. I believed the Holy Spirit was in me, but I had no personal evidence of his activity. My prayer was labored and definitely not inspired. The scripture was not laid open to the eyes of my mind. Prophecy and healing were words in a book, not realities. And worse, since I seemed to be overcome with sins and problems, I couldn't honestly say the Holy Spirit was overcoming them for me.

Like many Christians, I was thinking and behaving as a stepchild of the Galatians, rather than as God's son. Paul called the Galatians foolish, for they who had once experienced the marvels of the Holy Spirit, had now returned to mere self-help: "Did you receive the Spirit by works of the law, or by hearing with faith? Are you so foolish? Having begun with the Spirit, are you now ending with the flesh? Did you experience so many things in vain?—if it really is in vain? Does he who supplies the Spirit to you and works miracles among you do so by works of the law, or by hearing with faith?" (Gal 3:2-5). Paul was endeavoring to bring the Galatians back to normal Christianity by arguing from their experience. He reminded them that when they had yielded to the Holy Spirit by faith, his power flowed freely in their lives. Subsequently, when they attempted to make it on their own, while the Holy Spirit remained with them, he was bottled up. The result for the Galatians, and for any of their unhappy stepchildren, is subnormal Christian living.

The Holy Spirit is a reservoir of living water in all who believe in Christ. God wants this living water to flow into every nook and cranny of our lives. Jesus proclaimed, "If any one thirst, let him come to me and drink. He who believes in me, as the scripture has said, 'Out of his heart shall flow rivers of living water.'" Now this he said about the Spirit, which those who believed in him were to receive (Jn 7:37-39).

I had (and perhaps you have also?) performed what ought to have been an impossible feat. I stored up the Holy Spirit behind a man-made dam. Or, more to the point, I bottled up a river of living water and nearly died of thirst.

I have learned the lesson Paul was hammering home to the Galatians. The energy of the Holy Spirit is released in us when we yield to him in faith. The normal Christian life is one that is inspired, formed and directed by the Holy Spirit in us.

Power to Change

Detailing his manifold activity is beyond the scope of this book.[11] There is one fact, however, that I want to single out. People who yield to the Holy Spirit experience change, sometimes dramatically, in areas that have been obstacles. Anna, a dedicated Christian woman who died several years ago, provides a good illustration. Her husband had died suddenly, leaving her with four young children to raise. She never remarried; her whole life was spent generously caring for her offspring. Anna was a woman of great, simple faith, and she did many things well. But getting angry was one thing she did not do well. She had to grapple with repressed anger, irritability, occasional outbursts, and above all, resentments. I don't think it unfair to say that anger was her biggest problem.

Anna was the youngest daughter in a large Italian family, a factor that occasioned much of the anger that plagued her last years. In the old world customs, preserved in her family, daughters never left home until they married. But both of Anna's daughters left home when they turned twenty to pursue careers and Anna resented it profoundly. Her abiding anger flared up now and then, adding more tension to relationships that were already strained.

Anna's body was racked with cancer for a year before she died. Shortly after it was diagnosed, she and all of her children prayed that the Holy Spirit would be released in her life. They may have hoped that when she yielded to the Spirit in faith she would be healed of the disease. The cancer in her body did not subside—but the anger that gnawed at her and poisoned her relationships with her daughters was completely cured. A lady who had for years been angry just below the surface, became fundamentally peaceful. No one had to persuade her or counsel her. She just changed, and grace alone accounts for that. Before she died, she spent several happy months enjoying her renewed relationships with her daughters.

Not all personal change comes as dramatically as Anna's but the principle and the source of transformation for Christians is the same Holy Spirit.

TEN

Relationship Therapy

Living in the body of Christ is another major source of personal change for Christians. The body of Christ is a New Testament name for the system of relationships that exist among the men and women who have been incorporated into Christ. Paul described this reality in his letter to the Romans: "For as in one body we have many members, and all the members do not have the same function, so we, though many, are one body in Christ, and individually members one of another" (Rom 12:4-5). The body of Christ refers both to the entire Christian people as well as to the local Christian community.

Simply living with this set of relationships can produce considerable relief from emotional problems and improvement in the use and care of the emotions. Healthy personal relationships with other Christians is the active ingredient that generates emotional health. New Testament principles such as commitment, encouragement, forgiveness, forbearance and correction are among the elements of this process, which could be aptly called relationship therapy.

I know many people whose emotional lives

changed for the better when they became associated with churches or Christian groups that placed a high priority on the development of sound Christian relationships among members. Vince, for example, struggled for thirteen years with a problem of low self-esteem. Guilt feelings and a false sense of humility combined to prevent him from using his gifts, some of which were very obvious, to serve with confidence in his local congregation. His participation in a charismatic renewal prayer group was the main factor that helped him to overcome this emotional difficulty. He credits the expressed affection, encouragement, and committed relationships of the prayer group with changing his negative self-evaluation.

A Prescription for Change

Relationship therapy works for anger, too, as the following account shows. Carol, who was the mother of seven and had been very active in her church, tried for a number of years to overcome her difficulties with anger. When something angered her, she internalized it. Her husband Tom says that he never knew Carol was angry until the accumulated rage would explode over some minor incident. Carol tried to change, but for all her hard work, she improved only slightly. When Tom changed jobs, they moved to another city, where they became members of a Christian community.

After several years in the community, Carol found that she was having much less difficulty with anger. "I was surrounded by people," Carol explains, "who asked me to forgive them when they did something wrong. And when I offended somebody, they had the kindness to tell me about it. People in the community had a commitment to work out differences. When they got angry they let you know about it. Their love for me and their whole way of relating nudged me into changing and helped me to do it."

Not everyone who participates in a church or Christian group finds that his emotional difficulties simply disappear or come under control. The fact is that most local churches in our technological age are set up as organizations that offer services. They model themselves on other modern social agencies that place primacy on programs and activities rather than on sound personal relationships. Even members of relationship-oriented churches sometimes do not experience their emotional life improving. They may resist change or their emotional problems may have grown to proportions that require special attention.

The New Testament Strategy

If you have ever wondered what the New Testament has to say about the emotions, you may have discovered that it does not say as much about them as we modern Christians would like. It talks about the emotions here and there, but there is no place in all of scripture where the emotions are dealt with in an extensive way. People in the cultures in which the scriptures were written did not share the contemporary notion that all meaning in life depends upon the emotions. It is not that the people in the New Testament church were unemotional. I have already pointed out that they were emotionally more expressive than people in Western society today. And it is not that they did not have to learn to handle their emotions. But they understood their emotions from a different perspective; they handled them without centering their attention on them.

The process of emotional change that I call relationship therapy applies the New Testament teaching on emotions. When the New Testament discusses emotions, it does not deal with them so much in themselves but as they relate to behavior. Clearly, the best way to handle emotions is to be primarily concerned about righteous behavior.

For example, in chapter 4 of Ephesians Paul is concerned not so much with the emotional reaction of anger but with what the Christian does in response to it. "Be angry but do not sin. Do not let the sun go down on your anger, and give no opportunity to the devil" (Eph 4:26-27). In other words, people are going to get angry. When they do, they should be sure that their response is righteous.

The New Testament does not devalue or disregard feeling, but subordinates it to righteous action. It is interested more in our conduct than in our reactions, more on what we *do* than in how we *feel*. To state a contemporary slogan in reverse, we could say that the New Testament approach to the emotions is: If the right thing does not feel good, do it anyway.

It follows that a Christian who wants his emotions to help him live the Christian life will benefit more from placing the highest priority on loving others than from focusing on the emotion itself. The more we fuss about our problem with anger, the more we are preoccupied with it, the more we think about it, reflect on it, analyze it—the more it may come to dominate us. And the more it may resist change. Not that some self-understanding of our emotional difficulties isn't helpful, but a little goes a long way. The New Testament teaches that the more attention we pay to building healthy Christian personal relationships the healthier our emotional life will be.

The following story about Bill illustrates this point, in particular with regard to anger. Once, during my time as faculty adviser to the local InterVarsity Christian Fellowship, several members burst excitedly into my office to tell me that in the wee hours of the morning, some dorm students had made a commitment to Christ. Among those new Christians, was Bill, who happened to be in my Western Civilization course. An aggressive young man, Bill was pressing some very hard questions. The students asked me if I would be willing to talk with him. Over the next few years I got to know Bill very well. As a teenager, he had become so deeply mired in his feelings that he was hospitalized for psychosomatic illnesses during part of his senior year in high school. He had lived in radical subjectivity and followed his desires into every kind of immorality. One of his biggest difficulties was with anger that quickly escalated into fury. At one point, his parents found him a summer job several hundred miles from home, because of his inability to control this emotion.

I taught Bill many things about the Christian life in those years, but the truth that changed him the most was the first thing we discussed. Bill was very earnest about becoming a Christian. In his eagerness, he wanted to change himself all at once. And when everything did not change immediately, he got frustrated. One day, when he was stewing about this, I opened the New Testament to Matthew's gospel and read to him Jesus' response to the question put by the lawyer, "Teacher, which is the greatest commandment in the law?" "And he said to him, 'You shall love the Lord your God with all your heart, and with all your soul, and with all your mind. This is the great and first commandment. And a second is like it, you shall love your neighbor as yourself'" (Mt 22:34-39). We talked a while about what these commandments meant—about living entirely for God and in the service of brothers and sisters in Christ.

I have never seen anyone seize upon a truth and pursue it so ruthlessly as Bill did. Over a five-year period he learned how to yield to God, and he schooled himself in building and repairing personal relationships. The question, "What is the loving thing to do now?" displaced the self-concern and preoccupation with his feelings that had been at the forefront of his mind. As concern for righteous behavior became his habitual response, he became progressively freer from the emotional problems that had afflicted his teenage years.

In particular, he experienced much less difficulty with anger. In the past a considerable amount of his anger had stemmed from the wreckage in his personal relationships. He got angry at people who offended him; he got angry at himself for having behaved badly. After becoming a Christian, Bill eliminated his offensive behavior and made it a priority to relate well to people, and so a main root of his anger withered.

The key to all emotional wholeness—the secret to freedom from control by powerful emotions like anger—lies in placing preeminent concern on conducting our personal relationships righteously and getting our feelings to support us in the effort.

ELEVEN

How To Get Angry
the Right Way

Anger is supposed to be a useful emotion, one that supports our Christian lives. Unfortunately, for many of us, anger is not our servant but is rather a slave master. It has become something that leads us into sin or plunges us into depression. As we have seen, this condition need not persist. By the power of the Holy Spirit and the strength that comes from Christian personal relationships, an angry Christian can change fundamentally. The Lord wants us to be characteristically peaceful, so that we can respond righteously and with love in every situation.

We all need to be transformed by yielding to the Holy Spirit and living in the body of Christ. We also need to learn how to get angry in the right way. If your experience is similar to mine, you will understand that being baptized in the Spirit or living in a community church does not guarantee that we will always handle anger correctly. We need wisdom in responding to the angry reaction we feel inside. Grace and right relationships can change our angry responses so that we can get angry without sinning.

There is a threefold strategy for handling anger in a particular situation: (1) Do not repress anger; (2) Express it righteously; (3) Settle things quickly. This is a biblical approach, conforming to the pattern in Paul's instruction to the Ephesians: (1) Be angry; (2) Do not sin; (3) Do not let the sun go down on your anger (Eph 4:26).

Do Not Repress the Anger

Be angry. That seems to be a scriptural command. The wisdom behind it should be obvious. Pushing anger down fails to deal with it. The force that may do a great deal of damage when released in a fit of temper may do equivalent damage when repressed. The angry reaction does not dissipate but is expressed as cold anger and depression, internalized mirror images of hot anger and loss of control. While hot anger is no more or less righteous than cold anger, it is easier to deal with. The person who expresses his anger knows what he's dealing with and so does everyone around him. Repressed, indirectly expressed anger, however, is very hard to handle.

The repressed angry person falls into subtle wrongdoing: he avoids people, giving others "the silent treatment," deliberately reneges on responsibilities, spouts negative jokes, and acts out of self-pity. Often he does not realize that his actions result from repressed anger. His behavior may bewilder his immediate associates: What is going on? Did I do something wrong? Neither the angry person nor his associates are in a position to resolve the problem.

My file contains a letter from a friend that is to the point here. Patti explains how repressing her anger affected her and how she began to change it.

"As a child I got angry a lot, threw a lot of tantrums. As I grew older I kept it all inside, except at home (ask my folks!). When I came into Christian community even that outlet was taken away....All of this anger had to come out some way—and there was lots of it. Often it came out in situations totally unrelated to the one that originally made me angry. I felt I shouldn't get angry so I kept it in, until I couldn't keep it in any longer. I'd get irritated or react subtly in a not-so-loving way to a situation that ordinarily wouldn't have made me angry. It was always subtle and a lot of times people didn't know what was going on—they weren't even sure I had done anything wrong. I think women especially pick it up (which can be uncomfortable if you live with a group of Christian women, as I do). I realized that the anger I repressed was affecting my relationships with others.

"One of my close friends helped me identify the sources of my anger and to see the truth about these things. She also encouraged me to let my anger out as soon as it was there—and if I sinned in the process, to repent for the action. She assured me that this approach would be better than having the anger sit there and eventually seep out and poison my relationships. This way I had an opportunity to let my friends know what was really going on. I haven't totally overcome this difficulty, but now that I understand what is happening and am able to let my anger out, I am getting on top of it much faster."

Unrighteous as it is, even losing one's temper at least offers the chance for immediate repentance and repair. Pushing anger down out of reach sets us up for unredressed wrongdoing. But losing our temper is not the necessary alternative to bottling it up inside. We can let it out without sinning.

Express Anger Righteously

Do not sin. Anger does not have to be let out in bursts of temper nor does it have to impel us to do harm to ourselves or others. When anger rises in us in response to wrongdoing, we can address the situation and make the people involved aware of our anger.

In fact, Christians would integrate anger more effectively into their lives if they allowed themselves to get angry more. The main problem for Christians is not too much anger, but too little. We do not get angry enough at the right objects. I live in a town that flaunts its sin; as a city we would get high marks on all the New Testament lists of wrongdoing that merits the wrath of God. Idolatry, adultery, murder, and all their perverse companions—you name it and our town has it to the nth degree.

What do you suppose is the most common cause of the anger Christians experience as they drive around this city? I'd guess the unavailability of parking spaces, long traffic lights, and other inconsiderate drivers—in that order. We become angrier over inconveniences and failure to get our own way than we do over the numerous public offences that provoke the judgment of God. Expressing more overt anger for the right reasons will go a long way toward helping us get anger to be our servant.

When it's inappropriate to express anger directly, we can channel our anger constructively into determination to have things change, endurance, forbearance, or readiness to fight past the obstacle. All these expressions of anger have already been discussed.

Whatever the object of an angry reaction, we must be in control of how we express our anger if it is to be righteous anger. It is possible to communicate anger with great force and effect without losing one's temper. We must repent for uncontrolled anger, but not for anger over wrongdoing, vigorously expressed but under control.

Settle Things Quickly

"Don't let the sun go down on your anger, and give no opportunity to the devil" (Eph 4:27). Some people have asked me how literally they should take this injunction to clear up unrighteous angry exchanges before going to sleep. My response has been to encourage people to take it for what it says. Christians are always well-advised to settle disputes and quarrels as quickly as possible. If unrighteous behavior or anger rooted in hostility are allowed to settle in, they can easily destroy relationships. They won't simply disappear. Unrepentant wrongdoing accumulates poison like a festering abscess. Early and expeditious attention to the infection is the best medicine. The sooner we deal with disruptions in our relationships the easier it will be to control and channel our anger.

A large body of scriptural teaching exists that deals with repairing broken relationships. However, beyond my exhortation to repair wrongs quickly, I cannot present the whole teaching here.

Willpower Is Not Enough

It can seem contradictory to tell people to control their anger or channel it constructively, after advising them not to repress it. Repression is strictly a willpower approach to the emotions. When we're having an undesirable reaction, we get in there and gut it out. The human will has a lot of muscle, but not enough to discipline the emotions by itself. The strategy I recommend has more clout. You cannot express anger under control or channel it into patience without exercising your will. But the will is not the sole agent. Our partner in the process of getting anger to work right is the Holy Spirit. When we recognize this central fact, we are able to deal with anger more freely, without the tension that occurs when we try to muster our will to subdue it.

Christians who actively discipline emotions such

as anger are exercising the authority they have as sons and daughers of God. Grasping this truth helps to dispel the idea that control or channeling is mere willpower or repression. The biblical definition of "son" includes the expectation that a son possesses and exercises his father's authority. When the owner of the vineyard sent his son to deal with the tenants, he was confident that they would see the father's authority in the son and obey him (Mt 21:37). Those who by faith in Jesus Christ have become sons and daughters of God have his authority and should exercise it in their lives.

Exercising authority conjures up visions of achieving things by sheer willpower. This need not be the case. I can exercise my authority as a son to control or direct my anger without having to use a forceful will. For example, if I am getting angry because I am not thinking correctly, I can exercise authority by remembering the truth. Suppose I suspect without any evidence that someone has deliberately done something to offend me. I can remind myself that I must always expect good and not suspect evil. Or if I am angry due to pressure, I can exercise authority by reviewing my priorities and altering my commitments. Neither of these activities involve repression or brute willpower. They are active approaches, stemming from my authority as a son of God.

I have distinguished between an angry reaction and our response and have talked about responding righteously or channeling our anger. Does this mean that whenever we express anger it ought to be deliberate and intentional? Definitely not. We could be tempted to believe that we're supposed to reflect carefully about each situation and decide meticulously on the right behavior. This will be the case only for a period of time as we retrain ourselves to express anger righteously. But the goal is to be able to become angry in the right way without thinking about it very much. When anger is working well in our lives, we should be able to express it instinctively in the right way. The truth about anger and the Holy Spirit will make it possible.

TWELVE

Holding On

Simply learning how to distinguish righteous from unrighteous anger will reduce the occurrence of the latter variety for many Christians. As we learn to express anger righteously or channel it constructively, we will be freed from emotional slavery.

Some people, however, will find only slight relief from the teaching I have presented thus far. For numerous Christians, anger remains a sizable and persistent problem. Instruction about anger, even when combined with superhuman efforts at constructively channeling it, will not solve their difficulties. Inappropriate reactions to good or neutral situations will still mushroom in them, drawing them to unrighteous behavior. They will still get angry for all the wrong reasons, and their anger will often career out of control.

Dealing with Problem Anger

Christians can deal effectively with problem anger and be delivered from its grip, but it takes more than simply understanding and restraining ourselves to respond righteously. Getting free of problem anger depends on identifying its causes. Once we find the root, we can lay the axe to it and end the problem.

Four common reasons why anger takes over in our lives are: (1) holding on to things, (2) resentment, (3) too much pressure, and (4) fears and inhibitions.

When the same circumstances always trigger our anger, the root of the anger probably consists of our grasping something we ought to be yielding to the Lord. Holding on to something is in fact the most common source of problem anger. We may want something very badly and be unwilling to let go. The ensuing struggle leads almost inevitably to frustration, fuming, and unrighteous anger. Causes for this type of anger can be obvious, as when someone becomes angry over the death of a close relative. Sometimes the cause is less obvious, as may be the case when someone is unwilling to accept failure.

In my responsibilities as a pastoral worker in the Christian community to which I belong, I have helped a number of couples—especially the husband—with anger occasioned by an unexpected pregnancy.

The wedding service in some Christian churches asks the couple to express their willingness to accept children as the fruit of the marriage union. Others pray that the couple will be fruitful and blessed with children. Most couples want children and anticipate family life with excitement. Overpopulation, inflation, and social pressure exert a strong influence on the couple to plan family size intelligently. Over the years things go according to plan. But just as the quiver seems quite full (and "full" is defined differently by each couple, of course), now and again another unexpected arrow is produced. Anger is not an uncommon reaction to an unanticipated, unplanned pregnancy. Mothers of two may be duly fearful of all that's involved in caring for three in diapers, and dread gives way quickly to anger. When news of the blessed event-to-be reaches husbands; who may have struggled with the sexual control required by natural family planning or who may have no obvious resources to provide for the newcomer, they may get angry at themselves, their wives, God and everybody else in sight.

Anger may be the normal first reaction in such a situation, but it should be channeled into determination or courage. For a number of people, I have seen it linger on, and result in depression. It can even unravel lives that were in fairly good order. In most of these cases, the husband, wife, or both, were holding on to something they should have surrendered to the Lord—perhaps their vision for their family; their plans for more leisure; their fear of what relatives or neighbors would think and say; or some selfishness, such as frustration over getting pregnant after having sacrificed sexual intercourse regularly.

It Can Be Terminal

This brand of problem anger can be a terminal moral disease. I have in mind Pam, the possessive mother in C.S. Lewis's *The Great Divorce*, whose anger over the death of her son, Michael, probably caused her to choose hell rather than let go. In this fantasy, Lewis has voyaged from hell to the outskirts of heaven. There he overhears a conversation between Pam, now dead and in ghostly form, and her brother, Reginald, who appears as a Bright Spirit to welcome her with one last chance to surrender to God. When Michael had died as a youth, Pam enthroned her anger in her mind, and from this seat it dominated all her behavior, inflicting pain on her husband, daughter, and mother. Let's eavesdrop with Lewis, just after Reginald has explained how wrong it was for her to keep a ten years' ritual of grief over Michael:

"Oh, of course. I'm wrong. Everything I say or do is wrong according to you."

"But of course," said the Spirit shining with love and mirth so that my eyes were dazzled, "That's what we all find when we reach this country. We've all been wrong! That's the great joke. There's no need to go on pretending one was right! After that we begin living."

"How dare you laugh about it? Give me my boy. Do you hear? I don't care about all your rules and regulations. I don't believe in a God who keeps mother and son apart. I believe in a God of love. No one has a right to come between me and my son. Not even God. Tell Him that to His face. I want my boy, and I mean to have him. He's mine, do you understand? Mine, mine, mine, for ever and ever."

"He will be, Pam. Everything will be yours. But not that way...."[12]

Earlier in the encounter, the Spirit had explained that the way for Pam to have Michael back was to learn to want someone else besides Michael. "It's only the little germ of a desire for God that we need to start the process." Lewis and his readers are lead away from this scene before Pam finally makes a decision. But, clearly, there is only a spark of a chance that she will yield.

Laying the Axe to the Root

When holding on is the root of problem anger, we can lay the axe to it by surrendering to the Lord. As the Lord comes into our lives, he takes authority more fully over what now belongs to him. Some areas seem to elude him at first; these are the things we are grasping for our own use and direction. Inevitably, he comes to claim them. We can make this task easier (easier for us, that is) by presenting these areas to him as we discover we're still hanging on to them.

In my first year of graduate school, I spent more time doing evangelism than my heavy load of studies would normally permit. I decided to forego the extra reading programs that my colleagues had undertaken to prepare themselves for oral exams that were to take place the next year. I figured that the Lord would get me through them, since I was working so hard for him. That spring, I didn't do well in an important course, and in the fall I failed the first round of exams. I was furious—I had never failed anything before. I was so angry with God that I stopped praying and decided that if he wasn't about to help me, I'd do it myself. This stupidity lasted many more unhappy months than I care to remember. I was not very pleasant to be around—just ask my wife, who was newly married to me at the time. I did not let go until a friend, in a moment of extreme frustration, exclaimed to me, "You're so proud of your sins you think the Lord isn't big enough to deal with them." That broke me and I surrendered. After a few months, the anger and turmoil subsided and I got on with living as a Christian under Jesus' lordship.

One practical way to yield to him is by approaching difficulties with an attitude of praise and thanksgiving. "Rejoice always," Paul exhorts the Thessalonians, "pray constantly, give thanks in all circumstances; for this is the will of God in Christ Jesus for you" (1 Thes 5:16-18). Humanly speaking, thanksgiving is the furthest thing from our mind when some failure or loss has made us angry. Yet thankfulness is the axe that can sever the root of the problem.

I have already shared how a few years ago I was in the throes of frustration regarding my relationship with one of my children. I was so thoroughly disappointed with his behavior and my failures as his father that I was consumed with anger. It was almost impossible for me to relate to him without losing my temper. In one fit of discouragement I described the situation to a friend, who advised me that the first thing I needed to do was to be thankful. "That's easy for him to say," I thought. "He's single." "Easier said than done," I replied with a snap. "Do it anyway," he urged. So I made it a daily practice to express thanks to the Lord for this difficult relationship with my son. After a while my anger was reduced to manageable proportions. I was able to direct it into determination to have the whole situation change. Being thankful had worked.

Problem anger that stems from holding on may not be pleasant to deal with. But if we approach it as an opportunity to surrender more fully to the Lord, it will leave us better off than we were before it arrived. If we find ourselves unable to control anger, we should ask the Lord to show us what it is we are holding on to or how we need to change. Thus, the Lord can use our problem anger to bring other problems to the surface and give us an occasion to resolve them. In the course of surrendering more fully to the Lord, we will not only bring our anger under control, but also replace weakness with strength as we tackle related problems.

THIRTEEN

Resentment, Pressure, Inhibitions

Among the roots of problem anger, in addition to holding on, are resentment, too much pressure, and related emotional problems such as fear and inhibition. Diagnosing the presence of any of these will help us to apply the correct prescription.

Resentment

Resentment is a special form of anger caused by holding a grudge against someone or something that we think has hurt us. A resentful person wants to soothe his own injury by injuring the offender. Linked with resentment are its deadly companions, hostility and malice, which actively seek to destroy people and things. These are the spiritual problems Paul is referring to when he warns us to handle anger so that we give no opportunity to the devil.

Resentment is like a poison we carry around inside us with the hope that when we get the chance we can deposit it where it will harm another who has injured us. The fact is that we carry this poison at extreme risk to ourselves.

I have a cleaning agent in my garage that is poisonous. The label on its plastic bottle warns that the poison is so corrosive that it may eat through its temporary container. Resentment differs only in that it will *surely* damage its carrier, perhaps even more than the one against whom harm is intended. It is a corrosive poison that erodes emotional health.

Resentment intrudes itself into our minds, where it does most damage. The resentful person nurses hurts, real or imagined, by reliving the painful event. They embellish the injury by guessing at motives and magnifying the hurt out of all proportion. Resentment causes us to plot and savor vindictive actions, which we may or may not carry out. We take perverse enjoyment in anticipating the harm we intend for someone who has hurt us. All of us have heard an angry child threaten, "If Dad thinks I'm stupid, I'll show him. I'll flunk everything, and then he'll be right when he calls me stupid!" The child expects to get pleasure out of getting back at his father, and the very thought of it is strangely pleasant.

Christians should not need to be persuaded that resentment is wrong. Plainly, it is a sin against Christian love (1 Cor 13:5). Nor does revenge have any place in us, for the Lord reserves vengeance to himself (Rom 12:19). The Lord wants us to repent of resentment and put it away. This is the injunction of texts like that in Ephesians: "Let all bitterness and wrath and anger and clamor and slander be put away from you, with all malice, and be kind to one another...(Eph 4:31-32). If a person harbors resentments, he should take them up one at a time, repent for them, cancel the grudge and set them aside.

If someone injures us, we need not let the act remain unredressed, where it can generate resentment. We should go to the other person and attempt to be reconciled. Correction, forgiveness and forbearance are all ways of repairing broken relationships among Christians. Jesus said: "If your brother sins, rebuke him, and if he repents, forgive him" (Lk 17:3). And Paul gave this instruction to the Colossians: "Put on then, as God's chosen ones...patience, forbearing one another and, if one has a complaint against another, forgiving each other; as the Lord has forgiven you, so you also must forgive" (Col 3:12-13). This biblical strategy for addressing disruptions works best in situations that focus on building relationships. It may not work at all in the secular environments where Christians find themselves.[13]

Actively guarding our thoughts safeguards us against resentment. "Whatever is true, whatever is honorable, whatever is just, whatever is pure, whatever is lovely, whatever is gracious, if there is any excellence, if there is anything worthy of praise, think about these things" (Phil 4:8). Paul could have continued: "Whatever is false, whatever is slanderous, whatever is malicious, if there is any suspicion, if there is any thought of revenge, refuse to think about these things." Taking an active approach to clear our mind of resentment can help us exercise our authority as God's sons and daughters. People who have made the effort to think righteously have experienced a quantum reduction of problem anger. It is a preventive medicine that works.

Too Much Pressure

Irritability is a form of problem anger that requires special attention. An irritable person is always on the verge of becoming angry, or he is perpetually angry just beneath the surface. His tone of voice warns all comers to, "Beware of the man." Irritability's boon companion is defensiveness, as in the expression, "I am not irritable!" usually growled through clenched teeth. People who are constantly irritable frequently believe that they are irritable by nature. Irritability is somehow seen to be an unchangeable character trait, an indelible mark, an irremediable state of being. This is a delusion. We should clear out the rubbish produced by rationalization and recognize irritability for what it is—a sin. The first step to getting free of irritability is to repent for it, just as a Christian would repent for any other wrongdoing.

Problem anger may be a by-product of too much pressure. When there are too many demands made of us, we are more tense and more susceptible to anger, especially irritability. Pressure has many sources—overcommitment, unrealistic deadlines, mental and emotional overwork, trying too hard, perfectionism. The solution to constant irritability often involves letting up and relaxing in some area of our lives.

Christians sometimes accumulate new commitments without sorting out and letting go of some they have previously made. There are more good things to do than any one Christian could ever undertake. The overcommitted Christian who has a problem with anger would do well to reorder and reduce his priorities. We should ask the Lord what commitments he wants us to maintain and then delete those things that we would simply like to do.[14]

Christians sometimes put pressure on themselves and those around them by insisting on very high standards. In some areas, we are harder on ourselves and others than God himself is. We should be strict when morality is at stake; we should stand with the Lord, firmly against all unrighteousness. But where achievement or order is the issue, we can reduce our expectations. An irritable person may find relief by deciding to accept lower standards. Everybody he associates with would be better off too.

I was once asked by the mother of a twenty-year-old son how she could stop being constantly angry with him. He told her she was always on his back, and he was right. Everything about him provoked her to anger. Some things he was doing were simply wrong, including drug abuse, immorality and some irresponsibility with money. He did average work in school, but she thought he could do much better. She did not like his taste in clothes, and she detested his long hair. She described his room as a "bear's den." I advised her to hold the line on the areas involving moral behavior: "Let him know," I said, "just where you stand on drugs and sex. Define the limits you expect as long as he's in your house and hold him to them." But I told her to lower her expectations in other areas. "Don't make an issue of grades, clothes, or his hair. Unless the health department threatens to quarantine your house, I wouldn't say much about his room."

Irritable Christians should take this approach to themselves as well. We may have to be satisfied with good rather than best. But it will be better for us to be thus rid of irritability.[15]

Fears and Inhibitions

Persistent anger is sometimes a symptom of other emotional problems. Fear and inhibitions, for example, are roots of anger because they prevent a person from acting confidently and decisively. An inhibited person is not free to respond in situations, because he is afraid. Externally, he may appear to be quiet and mild, even loving. Internally, his social failures and frustrations with others produce a tangle of hostilities, criticalness and resentment. More often than not, he feels this anger more toward others than himself.

When anger is the by-product of other emotional disorders, its correction depends on theirs. A person whose anger stems from inhibitions will not overcome frustration until he gets free of fearfulness. More needs to be said about the cure for fearfulness and inhibition than I can say without going too far afield. Suffice it to say that the determination to serve others ahead of ourselves and the formation of right Christian personal relationships are two powerful ingredients in the process. The point I am making is that some forms of anger will not change until other emotional difficulties that cause them are adequately resolved.

I want to conclude with a word of caution and hope. The hazard in instruction on emotional problems is that people will decide to concentrate on making the emotion itself work better. This is invariably a mistake, since focusing on a feeling puts it in a position of control. In order to apply the teaching, a person will have to pay more than ordinary attention to the emotion for a time. It is advisable not to fix on it so that it becomes our sole concern. Emotional well-being is the fruit of healthy Christian personal relationships. The primary cure for problem anger is righteous conduct in our relationships.

Our hope is grounded in the knowledge that our partner in pursuing human and spiritual maturity is the Holy Spirit. We could apply all our willpower and only make our anger worse. But at work in us is the same Spirit that comes from the one who raised the crucified Jesus to life. Can he not bring new life to these mortal bodies? Is he not strong enough to transform our anger?

Notes

1. David Viscott, The Language of Feelings (New York: Pocket Books, 1977), p.13.

2. Ibid, pp. 103-104.

3. Floyd Ruch, *Psychology and Life*, 7th ed. (Chicago: Scott, Foresman and Co., 1963), pp. 209-210, quoted in Jay E. Adams, *The Christian Counselor's Manual* (Grand Rapids, Michigan: Baker Book House, 1973), p. 351.

4. Calvin Stein, "Practical Pastoral Counseling," in Jules H. Masserman, *Handbook of Psychiatric Therapies* (New York: Jason Aronson, Inc., 1973), pp. 177-178, quoted in Adams, *The Christian Counselor's Manual*, p. 351.

5. Jane Howard, *Please Touch* (New York: Dell Publishing Co., Inc., 1971), p. 150.

6. Robert Young, *Young's Analytical Concordance to the Bible*, 22nd ed. rev. (Grand Rapids, Michigan: Wm. B. Eerdmans Publishing Co., 1970).

7. Both women submitted these stories to me simultaneously and independently of one another in response to a request I made for such accounts.

8. Benjamin Spock, *Baby and Child Care* (New York: Pocket Books, Inc., 1966), pp. 327-328.

9. See Peter S. Williamson's review article, "Will the Assertive Inherit the Earth?" *Pastoral Renewal*, vol. 4, no. 2 (August 1979): 12-15.

10. Robert E. Alberti and Michael L. Emmons, *Your Perfect Right: A Guide to Assertive Behavior*, 3rd ed. rev. (San Luis Obispo, California: Impact, 1978), p. 115.

11. If I have whet your appetite—or, better, made you

thirsty—you should read Steve Clark, *Baptized in the Spirit and Spiritual Gifts* (Ann Arbor, Michigan: Servant).

12. C.S. Lewis, *The Great Divorce* (New York: The Macmillan Co., 1946), pp. 92-93.

13. It is beyond the scope of this book to develop a nuanced teaching on relationships. Interested readers should see *Pastoral Renewal* (August 1976, September 1976, April 1977, May 1977, February 1978, August 1978); other books in the Living as a Christian Series; and the cassette album *Christian Personal Relationships* (Ann Arbor, Michigan: Servant).

14. On reordering priorities, see Jim McFadden's cassette "Reordering Our Priorities" (Ann Arbor, Michigan: Servant, 1973) and *Pastoral Renewal* (November 1976 and July 1978).

15. For more on how to adjust our expectations see Steve Clark, "Law and Grace," *Pastoral Renewal*, vol. 2, no. 5 (November 1977): 33-37.